gabardine
& *other poems*

shyamal bagchee

© 2004 Shyamal Bagchee
Except for purposes of review, no part of this book may be reproduced in any form without prior permission of the publisher.

We acknowledge the support of the Canada Council for the Arts for our publishing program.
We also acknowledge support from the Ontario Arts Council.

Cover design by Michael Crusz
Author photograph by Sumana Sen-Bagchee

National Library of Canada Cataloguing in Publication

Bagchee, Shyamal, 1945-
    Gabardine and other poems / Shyamal Bagchee.

ISBN 1-894770-14-5

1. Erotic poetry, Canadian (English) I. Title.

PS8603.A44G33 2004   C811'.6   C2004-902024-2

Printed in Canada by Coach House Printing

TSAR Publications
P. O. Box 6996, Station A
Toronto, Ontario M5W 1X7
Canada

www.tsarbooks.com

for ssb
poet, lover and birdwatcher
as always

these gestures in an alien tongue

> you are a riddle i would not unravel,
> you are the riddle my life comprehends.
> and who abstracts the marvel
> abstracts the story to its sorriest end.
> —josephine miles

contents

fore-verse
necessarily so *3*

one **touching tongues**
touching tongues *7*
because *8*
lesser slave lake, alberta:
      remembering "summertime" *9*
yin kuo *11*
c:\poems\heart.hrt *12*
prepositions *13*
holdin' unholden *14*
nocturne *16*
whiteout *17*
the breaks *18*

two **the fecund ditch**
spring and fall *21*
mono/lithic *22*
french postcard from dublin *23*
extempore effusions:
      upon visiting the cliffs of moher *24*
bride *26*
lenore fini paints *27*
professing poetry *28*
on seeing a sculpture *29*
sand beach, maine *30*
inscape magic *31*
spring sentiments *33*
paintpots, yellowstone park *34*

***three* gabardine**
faces: a letter *37*
anna louisa miracle:
   on the canal bank *40*
minding berries *42*
gabardine *44*
thinking homes *49*

coda
where are the animals? *53*

acknowledgements *55*

fore-verse

necessarily so

        and there it lies
        uncircumcised
        infolded
        in stubborn
        regression
        from light
        tight encased
        in an indolent
        refusal of meaning

        what one needs is
        a sharp something
        a rapier's edge
        to prise

        one needs that one line
        the fine ooze
        of bright blood

        split open
        the poem
        disembowel
        all that
        preserved
        pollen

                                    for all that
                                  IT'S STILL
                                  A LIE, ALIVE

one touching tongues

touching tongues

noisy thoughts
from my head
(yours too)
rudely intrude
upon our electric
erratic heart impulses

touching
tongue to tongue
is more satisfactory,
lucid articulation
in deepening silences

because

'cause coconuts were abundant
      on million green trees

'cause you sat next to me
      in that dingy hotel room

'cause you peered at my poems
      over my shoulder
      your breath on my neck

'cause you relished the whole lines
      and the bro
           ken ones, too,

'cause you were quiet when i read

'cause you noticed the fine print
      and the MAJUSCULE

'cause you asked me not to turn
      the pages too soon

'cause you learnt by heart
      a line or two

'cause the sun went down painfully red
      across kovalam bay
      and you knew when not to speak

'cause you were not there
      at day's end in kanyakumari

lesser slave lake, alberta: remembering "summertime"

this is land north of summer
here fall is spare, some deracinated poplars
self-consciously aglow
among the forbidding pointedness
of stubborn evergreens, these woods
change neither colour nor shape nor mood

s
  u
    m
      m
        e
          r
            t
              i
                m
                  e

is a song half a world
and many longings away,
the slim canal girl, the hopeful voice—

miracle images
linger and trail off
in a lushwet gully of the mind
someone tugs somewhere
at the folds of the cortex

all i really know is the tightening grip
on the steering wheel
while the straight road whizzes by
untold kilometres into
some inarticulable arctic north

and believe me
whether one is here or there
makes no inconsiderable difference

yin kuo

    the ginkgo grows
    luminous fruits
    silver smooth

    this i learned
    from you
    who have
    eaten them often
    in distant nanjing

    and surely
    the young tree
    we walked by
    had branches
    covered woolly
    white
    for me
    it's the textured
    leaf butterfly-
    split

    have you seen
    one floating
    cool green
    on dark pool
    above dappled
    goldfishes
    red and orange?

c:\poems\heart.hrt

heart less
less than
cup brimful
less than
brimming
less full than
less than full
cup to the brim
topped to brim
heart not held
hand empty
not cupped
unheld

unhanded   loss litany
less heart   heart litany
more hurt   hurt litany
heart loss   hurt heart
hurt more   little loss?
more loss   little heart?

none spilled
none topped
unspilt unspoilt
spoilt unspilt
hurt heart
hurt within
without heart
hurt without
and within

    [Tab][Tab]F12 → → Ctrl-F8,2,4,F6 **loss loss** [HRt]

prepositions

in a rainy boston
cattails sway
against the mist
around the pond
beside the runway

in his hand
he cupped her slimness

his cup ran over

holdin' unholden

white moon and goodbye
parking lot
hard pavement
and

for one bated instant

holding
and then only held
holden held
unheld

slim
as a stalk
of canal flower
buds of breasts
just opening
blooming
just

loveliness
girlslim
long hair
barely nuzzled

take care darling

and
keep
in
touch

one bated instant

and

one
lifetime

nocturne

over hedges, sanitary landfills
and the occasional knoll
barely scraping tops of cairns
he floated out real alone
under a slip of a melony moon
sliced thin

it's hard to know
if the night was misty
—surely not fog-some thick
except over meadow ponds
and the slight saulteaux creek
all crooked and in a shroud

past the hump of meru
they beamed him down
and washed his eyes
in malmsey wine;
his feet they covered
with cinnamon foam, on his tongue
they laid a ginger candy,
and sprinkled civet on his belly
the he-thing was tipped with ruby—
quite pointless, one must say

he woke up wednesday feeling fresh
and ready for work after restful sleep,
a bit perplexed to see the wife
all ruffled by silly erotic dreams,
and this only a midweek morning

whiteout

folks here call it a whiteout
it makes for peculiar luminous nights,
cotton gauze laden air connects
the snowed-in land with a pearly sky;
you don't see very far,
the moon, the stars are hidden

you don't sleep well either
for snow diffuses streetlights,
the whiteness is soaked up by the night;
even jolly northern light turns matronly
on a night as this
brooding glumly over the albino scene
this is the northern night—
pale light over a powdery landscape
white as a surgeon's glove,
milky as spilled semen
you know you are far from home
when you look at your ill-lit room,
the empties, and at made-up blondes on tv
whooping it up aprés ski
unmindful of the cold outside their chalet

home is where slow-hipped girls
play warm slippery games
with dusky lovers
in thatched huts,
on temple squares,
and lawns of suburban bungalows
when the nights are dark as kohl

the breaks

inez, listen—
when with supple succession
the little calamities flow in
like toe-numbing waves
at a favourite beach gone sour,

when ingrid and ingmar
importune like blind paramours—
and we, stopped at some fortuitous red light,
lean briefly over toward
an uncalled-for kiss,
—those are the breaks;

when at brief summer's gloomy end
the virginia creeper
on a neighbour's wall
abruptly turns bright crimson,
—that, too, is a break

two the fecund ditch

spring and fall

spring is not for lovers

it is too full of slender spiky things
stubborn shoots and fleshy mushroom growths
fast frothy waters and impatient loins

spring is abrupt and green and sharp

it is
random sowing of seeds
too much honey sucking

hectic begetting and slim spasmodic hips

give us warm odorous autumns
earthtones and gentle furrowed mounds
lazy tumescent worms on the brown soil
and bits of hay on slow pliant buttocks

long smothering embraces in chilly dawns
and stout shafts of corn and grains of ripe wheat

most of all grains of ripe wheat
unshod and swollen and cleaved
like shaven twats of goddesses on temple walls

mono/lithic

sensational
he cried amazed
as sun hit aslant
a thousand mica specs
encrusting the hillside
and there were
green things too

don't exaggerate
she said coolly
it's only plain quartz
plainly glittering
plainly rainbow-flecked
no more than plainly crimson
and green and orange and purple
overblown words are hardly better
than overelaborate feelings
her hand placed lightly
on his crotch she added
it's solid rock
of the soil really
and it makes sense

french postcard from dublin

hard to guess what fatal innocence
made her leave untouched
the wild hair in nymphet armpits;
it does not fit the picture

parted legs let slanted shafts of light
play between them (dazzling rays
caught in a cross-star lens);
the shutter cannot filter out
odour in the rumpled cushion,
wine is unclear in the dimestore goblet
and artful lipstick stain fails to distract

a dank insistent smell comes
from that print—
that room, that chintz bedspread,
the spreadeagled venus
with rouged nipples and candy breath

love has set its booth in a place of excrement

but somewhere in that snapshot
is a girl the viewfinder will not discover:
the scene it will not focus upon, a garden
much like the framed needlepoint on her wretched wall
a girl who slowly swings her hips like balzac's maids
and has frizzy armpits that smell of verbenas

extempore effusions:
upon visiting the cliffs of moher

at first it felt somehow ridiculous
hardly measuring up to the billing—
the way we arrived at land's end
scampering over fieldstone walls
panting up and down a hilly shore;
and lying prone on the flat ledge
faces projected over an absolute misty drop

still, the rock we lie on is invitingly warm
the slant rays of the western sun
grazing the ground it has just lost
embracing a continent in reluctant parting—
my loins feel that lingering desire

these, then, are the terminal cliffs
folding rock-walls lowered precipitously
into an impatient growling ocean
froth swirling in confined angular bay
white flecked and cloudy green

here gulls fly below us
dart and scream as we refocus memory
accommodating restless wings
within the unaccustomed bird's eye view
—below still is the passionate water
we would rather not acknowledge

but its rumble reaches our perch
through the rockbed
penetrates schizoid solitudes
and entering chest cavity
mixes with other thumps and noises,
shudder of sea informs trembling thighs
and hearts register seismic spasms

the mind insists on remaining unmoved
stubbornly holding eyes downcast
looking into troubling depths yet avoiding meaning
not glancing sideways—at someone else's wife—
nor fingers tracing inside of sunglistened lips
nor arms reaching out in an eager clasp
that would surely be most right
in this really terrific spot
overlooking the turbulent crotch of earth

bride

i came to your bed
a stranger from across the seas,
to disturb the repose of your suburban marriage
promising the madness of exotic lust;
it thrills me strangely to see
how these dark limbs awaken your memory
of a native betrothal;
from beyond years of complacent loving
you recall again the lithe brownness
and his fierce innocent longing

from the ashes of a marriage,
in a bed of incontinence,
come home in my unfamiliar arms
to your momentary true wedding
to the cree boy
who did not live to be seventeen

lenore fini paints

a long-nailed finger
slips under the garter
presses down firm flesh
hard eyes stare at a naked crotch;

the other, legs thrown askew
looks away—
martyr to uncopulable love;
lips part
as sphinctres tighten
aching for sharper pains;

tongues have swollen in their feverous mouths

professing poetry

        nothing but that old vehement, bewildering kiss
                                        —wby

it is difficult to explain even to oneself
why a seasoned professor, witty and aloof,
must secretly take to bed nubile images
of this or that young person whose face
stands out in the baffled crowd
listening to discourses on esemplastic imagination,
perform untold lechery on unsuspecting limbs
and engrave witless lips with ripening kisses

who knows if the lesson is done
till passion lights up eyes
that are ravishing and vacant,
and joy and filth and the opulent sapphire
glitter together in moist throbbing crotch

on seeing a sculpture

this is no goddess from khajuraho
in perfected bliss of celestial coitus;
what can the viewer say to this woman—
solitary, real, her thighs peeled back
tight mound of sex thrust in his face?

> perhaps she resolves herself,
> recuperating—claiming back her flesh
> for that alone is worth it all
> snatching herself into being
> out of a cave, a rockface,
> out of the brownness of earth
> or the inviting undulation of sea

one sees her dissolving too—
back into unbodied painlessness
pulled into undifferentiation
reluctant flesh still clutching onto shape
sharp collarbones plump breasts
hard nipples, gouged-out belly
and that cleaved erection between thighs—
she's going but not quite gone

> arriving or leaving—either way and both
> this is the most truth she makes us know:
> desire is good

sand beach, maine

toes feeling out edges
of steps they suspect are there,
my fingers in your cool hand
we climb down
to the dark beach below;

heavy sand shifts underfoot,
who knows how close is the water's edge—
the pillaging waves, though, are not far
nor their hissing spray

cutting wind, icicle spiked,
erodes all sober memory
of the familiar ordinary day;
quiet joys no longer suffice,
inconsequential
before the gritty necessity of touch
the embraces are hectic,
spasmodic, indelicate—
breasts sprout eloquent
into palms overcome by generosity;

silenced by the clamour
stony tongues wait caged
in clamped mouths

a beerbottle crashes
splintering
      the night;
and,   just for now,
the tide is contained

no promises made for a tomorrow

inscape magic

dearest woman with creampuff breasts
the rhythmic creaking of your suburban bed
is not the heartthrob of the land
nor does that land care much
for the sweaty man increasing his brood
of lawyers and lumberjacks
assorted mockheroes of his tribe
the alien lot he cranks
out of your generous womb

this vast and silent place
that you claim with charming arrogance
to be your very very own
hasn't had a pulsebeat in ages
its history older than that faded print
of your granddad scratching soil
for wheat coal and paydirt

to set magic afoot again
come secretly to some obscure valley
lie down at the centre
of a halftraceable medicine circle
strain your ears for echoes of ancient music
let sharp winds ravish your loosened hair
rub odorous herbs into the pale skin

dance dance
dance in the night
let flickering flames of lost ceremonies
revive the glorious urge that plumped your thighs
and swelled your nipples like budding crocuses

repossess the woman long squandered
among plastic lilacs of a honeymoon suite
moan delirious at your nakedness

> *you will hear the voice of the land*
> *and the soft earth will gladly take*
> *the imprint of your girlslim loveliness*

spring sentiments

keep me from fashions of hope
sentiments that hold, let's say
that spring supplants winter,
that arriving later the one
puts the other to rout

from what I know
of seasons and passions
that hardly seems true

but for
those rare in-between times
when piercing sleet of march
erases sedate january comforts
teaching forgetful nerves
new goosebumping tricks

my tongue digging into your belly
puckered nipples in freezing rain
and fierce wind whipping
stippling buttocks thighs
—making rainbows out of grey muck

and that, as we well know,
is a seldom happening

paintpots, yellowstone park

the blue one
aquamarine clear
doesn't do much for me
merely replicating
the sky when it's clear
it declaims
a derivative rhetoric
loudmouthed and flashy;
on overcast days
it is necessarily mute

but the ochre-tinted pool
is inexorable—
though you can bet
i try hard to ignore
its rivetting pull—
bubbling hot, mud-streaked
acrid and steamy
menstruating
hole in the ground
opens old wounds
peeling the scab
off cauterized arteries
of memory (and desire?
how can one be certain?)

three gabardine

faces: a letter

i

i saw you in a dream last night

in the uneasy sleep
of early hours just before sun-up,
close together by the lake
at badkal—our lips met
clumsy, eager, pretending surprise;
how long, shall we say,
it's been since our faces had
anything to do with each other?
or with the crisp air around badkal?
thirty years? more?

tourism department has stepped in since
a lot has changed, I hear,
improved in the civic interest—
liquor store and taxi stands,
restaurants with private booths, much else;
hardly my memory of the place,
the shore was rocky, and scrawny acacias
punctuating granite outcroppings
flowered only in the dry season

ii

there's a photo in my album—
i'm afraid not a faded one
the way it's supposed to be in a poem
been just too timid to look at it often—
you are in it, still smiling brightly; i am there, too,
a few others, and four faces no one will ever see again

time passes, people do as well;
you will scarcely call that news any more

iii

last month, during a dim winter weekend,
our bangla club celebrated saraswati puja,
following an alien calendar
in this frozen city of a northern continent;
halfway through the community dinner
a young woman had to be rushed
to the maternity ward—
both mother and child are doing well—
our only sign of spring this season

i have no other news to send
but tell me, do school children
still stay up all night before puja
cutting up fruits for the goddess
and making chains of coloured paper?
as i look out of my window
at the swirling snow on the ledge
and at the solid river below,
somehow these become urgent questions
the empty lots behind your father's house
where we set up tent for worship and frolic,
have developers got to them
and built offices and video arcades?

it was good to have run into you
on that otherwise unremarkable
visit to delhi some years back,
thought you looked a bit tired

years ago you broke a leg on the playground
the school bus made an extra trip
to bring you home at an unusual hour,
i wonder if it still hurts

iv

perhaps you know that father
died last autumn—
i was at safeway
flinching at the price
of papayas imported from fiji
when they paged me—
odd; his favourite fruit,
i hardly ever touch the stuff

two days later, in an entirely familiar city
i cremated him, nothing less familiar then;
now little else is more vivid

when I immersed his ashes,
thousand durga images were floating down the jamuna
another dusshera was over

v

it has snowed all night
a pile has drifted high against my door
impassable
i better go and shovel a path through,
or the mailman will stay away
it's good to do hard work in middle age
the body stays firm
the mind, however, is another matter

my lips retain a faint feel of yours

anna louisa miracle:
on the canal bank

>and the cut of her! and the strut of her!
>— joyce

and so—
the road whizzes by
one hundred and sixty-seven miles
due north
straight as conviction
undulating as a prone girl
taut skin dew-wet
shimmering

at fifty-six or so degrees north
one need give nor take
any latitude

but an hundred and eight
sharp longitudes sever us—
the flowermantled
midsummer's spring child
met by some lazy canal
among cattails and fernfronds
in some impossible near-far
august hour

with gentle reassuring words
she resolutely claimed
my hesitant verses
aching half truths and impossible maybes

miraculous audience and
cool respondent,
those intemperate mutterings
and these, are for you—
to be or not to be

minding berries

mountain ash berries—
she doesn't care for them,
my wife

always out of season,
never quite what she expects,
mountain ash berries
always out of place

before even one leaf has touched gold
their colour turns to crimson,
announcing, when she least wants to hear,
the winter's wail while it's still
summer green everywhere

and in the all-white
of northern freeze-up
they hang on barren limbs
of sickly trees
like barely congealed blood—
blotches of scarlet
in the sterile snowscape
my wife, she can't stand them—
red mountain ash berries

well, i have no real feelings for them;
but once set to thinking
mountain ash berries
vaguely bring back
a misty morning
seven steps around a small fire,
few dancing reddish flames,
perhaps also a bit of vermilion
that had something, i think,
to do with us
one otherwise chilly dawn in bengal

gabardine

chilly sea air
merely an excuse
I gave you my plastic
windbreaker
to wear
taiwanese
recycled polymer
pulled out of the trunk
crumpled khaki grey
for in distant maine
the slant afternoon light
made your singular style
lunge at me
at an odd
throbbing angle
no relief till
darkness fell
on our ways
separate

      (the double GG
      on the baseball cap
      of the only freshman who
      will probably get a B+
      on this poetry exam
      does not stand for
      brad from a farm
      near saskatchewan river
      crossing)

your soft jean jacket
rounding out
slight shoulders
pert breasts
stung sharp
as did
smooth gabardine
slacks rich
to the touch—but
that came later
briefly
in the night
now run together
in time's confusion

       (why won't sprinklers
       go off
             right now
       and slick down styled hair
       crisply fresh with youth
       unfurl knitted brows
       splatter on dubious
       sullen faces
       interro
             gating
       pleasure of articulate
       phrases, petulant)

and also the texan
boots stunning
ornate to the knee
yellowed with
ease of years
the tooled leather
arrogantly beckoned
my fingers curled
into my palms
deprived

        (at term end
        the overhead projector
        sits on the floor
        useless unplugged
        chained to the
        lectern—
        and they write
        miserably
        about poets, lovers
        birdwatchers
        "the slow movement seems
        somehow
        to say much more"
        and wait for the clock
        to call off
        the suffering
        inflicted by splendid
        efficient words—
        not theirs
        who wear stray
        dog cantina
        teeshirts)

the desperate trick
then
was to even you out
make tolerable in
oversized mantle from
bargain basement
put a stop
to allure

all the time
i mostly wanted
to wrap the whole
naked you
slim hips
long arms
in creamy tussore

just now
i wish only
that you were
here, in gabardine
my face on the
heavy fabric
against your thigh

       (the only bright face
       in this room
       has carrot-red hair
       dyed too bright
       and misspells
       rhythm)

much of what I feel
is frag
        mentally
scattered over dark fields
sharp u-turns on hillsides
and day and night
i dodge the jagged bits
too little
summed up
as love

(and lust, too,
is a word
i might need)

thinking homes

trying to touch you
with you gone so far away
i have turned the soil in your
strawberry patch, watered
the houseplants & monitored
filtered light on the african violet
washed all your cardigans
in the kitchen sink
and not pulled out a
single strand of black hair
tangled into each one of them
i have trellised your clematis
broomed the garage floor
smelt each new clustre on your
lilac bush; every night i've
built fresh sandwiches for
our moody teenager's school lunch
and in the long evenings
thinned out the tiny apples
and pinched off deadheads
from beds of irises and tulips
watching the thick leaves
on the sigvaldasons' manitoba maples
glisten in the fiery light of
reluctant prairie sunsets

the fuzzy chinese poppies
are readying to let loose
their crinkly orange blooms
already pink is bursting
through tight peony buds

i have to stop kidding
myself—come back
i want to touch your lips

> ps: I do hope the mimosas by the rickshaw tracks and the crimson-canopied *shimul* are comforting you a whole lot better; you were so keen to go 'home'

coda

where are the animals?

my zoo-keeper discourses
wondrously down cinnamon
lanes, tobacco splattered
and twisted
across towns
and palm-thatched villages;

why harass subpoenaed
stars pasted on the
lagoon's face?
what is simpler
than green graffiti
on brown bosoms and buttocks
among coriander and maize?

something ruptures
between legs, lips
the same thing

        i am yet to find the animals
        for her cage

Acknowledgements

Early versions of some of the poems in this book first appeared in these journals:

Canada: *ARIEL: A Review of International English Literature, Secrets from the Orange Couch, The Toronto Review;*

India: *The Commonwealth Review, Journal of the Poetry Society of India;*

Singapore: *World Literature Written in English;*

USA: *Café in Space: The Anais Nin Literary Journal; New Press Literary Quarterly, Sevenoaks Journal, South Dakota Review;*

E-zine: *nasty.cx*

The quoted lines in the poem "Gabardine" are from Nissim Ezekiel's "Poets, Lovers, Birdwatchers" in his *Collected Poems 1952-1988* (Delhi: Oxford University Press, 1992).

The quotation on the dedication page is from the poem "Riddle" by Josephine Miles and is taken from her *Collected Poems 1930-83* (Urbana: University of Illinois Press, 1998). The Yeats quote for the epigraph on page 28 is from *Deirdre*; the Joyce quote on page 40 is from *Finnegan's Wake*.

Though balding rapidly, Shyamal Bagchee is an unrepentant romantic. This is his first book of poems; a second will appear shortly. His poetry has been published in literary journals internationally. He attended universities in Delhi, Santiniketan (Tagore's "poet's school"), Hamilton, Ontario, and Toronto. Shyamal Bagchee lives and writes in St Albert, Alberta. He loves driving very long distances on that province's uncrowded highways and biways. He is a keen and serious photographer.